Year 4 Assessing Pupil P n Mathematics (APP)
Photocopiable Activity Book

CW00449898

Introduction

Using the assessment statements outlined on the Primary National Strategy Assessing Pupils Progress Guidelines (reproduced under licence at the beginning of this book) this series of books provides carefully organised assessments for each area of the mathematics curriculum. The activities can be used to determine the level a pupil is working at. They can also be used to indicate gaps in learning.

There is a book for each year group from Year1 – Year 6 aimed at pupils aged 6 to 11. When a written test is completed, an easy to carry out assessment of AT1 (Using and Applying Mathematics) is provided to enable a National Curriculum level to be determined (e.g. Level 3b). The tests are compiled in such a way that a Level 3b would be exactly the same whether achieved on a Y1, Y4 or Y6 assessment.

For each year group there are differentiated assessments aimed at pupils of different abilities.

In this Year 4 book there are assessments for:

Level 2 = Lower Ability
Level 3 = Average Ability
Level 4 = Higher Ability

The assessments within this book can be used as a baseline test or used at the end of a term to assess progress.

Contents

Topical Resources publishes a range of Educational Materials for use in Primary Schools and Pre-School Nurseries and Playgroups.

Copyright © 2010 Helen Maden
First Published January 2010.
ISBN: 978-1-907269-14-1

Illustrated by John Hutchinson, Art Works, Fairhaven, 69 Worden Lane, Leyland, Preston

Designed by Paul Sealey, PS3 Creative, 3 Wentworth Drive, Thornton, Lancashire.

Printed in the UK for 'Topical Resources' by T. Snape and Co Ltd., Boltons Court, Preston, Lancashire.

For the latest catalogue
Tel 01772 863158
Fax 01772 866153
email: sales@topical-resources.co.uk

Visit our Website at:
www.topical-resources.co.uk

Mathematics Attainment Target 1 (MA 1) Using and Applying Mathematics

Level 4 (L4)

Problem solving

A develop own strategies for solving problems, e.g.
- make their own suggestions of ways to tackle a range of problems
- make connections to previous work
- pose and answer questions related to a problem
- check answers and ensure solutions make sense in the context of the problem
- review their work and approaches

B use their own strategies within mathematics and in applying mathematics to practical context
- use mathematical content from levels 3 and 4 to solve problems and investigate

Communicating

A show understanding of situations by describing them mathematically using symbols, words and diagrams, e.g.
- organise their work from the outset, looking for ways to record systematically
- decide how best to represent conclusions, using appropriate recording
- begin to understand and use formulae and symbols to represent problems

Reasoning

A search for a solution by trying out ideas of their own, e.g.
- check their methods and justify answers
- identify patterns as they work and form their own generalisations/rules in words

Level 3 (L3)

Problem solving

A select the mathematics they use in a wider range of classroom activities, e.g.
- use classroom discussions to break into a problem, recognising similarities to previous work
- put the problem into their own words
- use mathematical content from levels 2 and 3
- choose their own equipment appropriate to the task, including calculators

B try different approaches and find ways of overcoming difficulties that arise when they are solving problems, e.g.
- check their work and make appropriate corrections, e.g. decide that two numbers less than 100 cannot give a total more than 200 and correct the addition
- begin to look for patterns in results as they work and use them to find other possible outcomes

Communicating

A begin to organise their work and check results, e.g.
- begin to develop own ways of recording
- develop an organised approach as they get into recording their work on a problem

B discuss their mathematical work and begin to explain their thinking, e.g.
- use appropriate mathematical vocabulary
- talk about their findings by referring to their written work

C use and interpret mathematical symbols and diagrams

Reasoning

A understand a general statement by finding particular examples that match it, e.g.
- make a generalisation with the assistance of probing questions and prompts

B review their work and reasoning, e.g.
- respond to 'What if?' questions
- when they have solved a problem, pose a similar problem for a partner

Level 2 (L2)

Problem solving

A select the mathematics they use in some classroom activities, e.g. with support - find a starting point, identifying key facts/relevant information
- use apparatus, diagrams, role-play, etc. to represent and clarify a problem
- move between different representations of a problem, e.g. a situation described in words, a diagram, etc.
- adopt a suggested model or systematic approach
- make connections and apply their knowledge to similar situations
- use mathematical content from levels 1 and 2 to solve problems and investigate

Communicating

A discuss their work using mathematical language, e.g. with support
- describe the strategies and methods they use in their work
- engage with others' explanations, compare... evaluate...

B begin to represent their work using symbols and simple diagrams, e.g. with support
- use pictures, diagrams and symbols to communicate their thinking, or demonstrate a solution or process
- begin to appreciate the need to record and develop their own methods of recording

Reasoning

A explain why an answer is correct, e.g. with support
- test a statement such as, 'The number twelve ends with a 2 so 12 sweets can be shared equally by 2 children'

B predict what comes next in a simple number, shape or spatial pattern or sequence and give reasons for their opinions of objects, shapes or numbers

Mathematics Attainment Target 2 (MA 2) Number and Algebra

Level 4 (L4)

Numbers and the number system
A recognise and describe number patterns, e.g.
- continue sequences involving decimals

B recognise and describe number relationships including multiple, factor and square

C use place value to multiply and divide whole numbers by 10 or 100

...percentages, & ratio
A recognise approximate proportions of a whole and use simple fractions and percentages to describe these
- recognise simple equivalence between fractions, decimals and percentages e.g. 1/2, 1/4, 1/10, 3/4
- convert mixed numbers to improper fractions and vice versa

B order decimals to three decimal places

C begin to understand simple ratio

...between them
A use inverse operations, e.g.
- use a calculator and inverse operations to find missing numbers, including decimals
- 'undo' two-step problems
- understand 'balancing sums' including those using division, such as 20 + ___ = 100 ÷ 4

B understand the use of brackets in simple calculations

C quickly derive division facts that correspond to multiplication facts up to 10 × 10

Solving numerical problems
A solve problems with or without a calculator
- solve two-step problems choosing appropriate operations
- deal with two constraints simultaneously
- interpret a calculator display of 4.5 as £4.50 in context of money
- carry out simple calculations involving negative numbers in context

B check the reasonableness of results with reference to the context or size of numbers

C begin to use simple formulae expressed in words

D use and interpret coordinates in the first quadrant

Written methods
A use efficient written methods of addition and subtraction and of short multiplication and division e.g.
- calculate 1202 + 45 + 367 or 1025 - 336

B add and subtract decimals to two places

C multiply a simple decimal by a single digit, e.g.
- calculate 36.2 × 8

Level 3 (L3)

Numbers & the number system
A understand place value in numbers to 1000, e.g.
- represent/compare numbers using number lines, 100-squares, base 10 materials, etc.
- recognise that some numbers can be represented as different arrays
- use understanding of place value to multiply/divide whole numbers by 10 (whole number answers)

B use place value to make approximations .

C recognise negative numbers in contexts such as temperature .

D recognise a wider range of sequences, e.g.
- recognise sequences of multiples of 2, 5 and 10

Fractions and decimals
A use simple fractions that are several parts of a whole and recognise when two simple fractions are equivalent, e.g.
- understand and use unit fractions such as 1/2, 1/4, 1/3, 1/5, 1/10 and find those fractions of shapes and sets of objects
- recognise and record fractions that are several parts of the whole such as 3/4, 2/5
- recognise some fractions that are equivalent to 1/2

B begin to use decimal notation in contexts such as money, e.g.
- order decimals with one dp, or two dp in context of money
- know that £3.06 equals 306p

Operations, relationships....
A derive associated division facts from known multiplication facts, e.g.
- given a number sentence, use understanding of operations to create related sentences, e.g. given 14 × 5 = 70, create 5 × 14 = 70, 70 ÷ 5 = 14, 70 ÷ 14 = 5, 14 × 5 = 10 × 5 add 4 × 5
- use inverses to find missing whole numbers in problems such as 'I think of a number, double it and add 5. The answer is 35. What was my number?'

B begin to understand the role of '=', the 'equals sign, e.g.
- solve 'balancing' problems such as 7 × 10 = 82 - ___

Mental methods
A add and subtract two-digit numbers mentally, e.g.
- calculate 36 + 19, 63 - 26, and complements to 100 such as 100 - 24

B use mental recall of the 2, 3, 4, 5 and 10 multiplication tables, e.g.
- multiply a two-digit number by 2, 3, 4 or 5
- understand finding a quarter of a number of objects as halving the number and halving again
- begin to know multiplication facts for ×6, ×8, ×9 and ×7 tables

Solving numerical problems
A use mental recall of addition and subtraction facts to 20 in solving problems involving larger numbers, e.g.
- choose to calculate mentally, on paper or with apparatus
- solve one-step whole number problems appropriately
- solve two-step problems that involve addition and subtraction

B solve whole number problems including those involving multiplication or division that may give rise to remainders, e.g.
- identify appropriate operations to use
- round up or down after simple division, depending on context

Written methods
A add and subtract three-digit numbers using written method, e.g.
- use written methods that involve bridging 10 or 100
- add and subtract decimals in the context of money, where bridging is not required

B multiply and divide two digit numbers by 2, 3, 4 or 5 as well as 10 with whole number answers and remainders, e.g.
- calculate 49 ÷ 3

Level 2 (L2)

Numbers & the number system
A count sets of objects reliably, e.g.
- group objects in tens, twos or fives to count them

B begin to understand the place value of each digit, use this to order numbers up to 100, e.g.
- know the relative size of numbers to 100
- use 0 as a place holder
- demonstrate knowledge using a range of models/images

C recognise sequences of numbers, including odd and even numbers, e.g.
- continue a sequence that increases or decreases in regular steps
- recognise numbers from counting in tens or twos

Fractions
A begin to use halves and quarters, e.g.
- use the concept of a fraction of a small quantity in a practical context such as sharing sweets between two and getting ½ each, among four and getting ¼ each
- work out halves of numbers up to 20 and beginning to recall them

B relate the concept of half of a small quantity to the concept of half of a shape, e.g.
- shade one half or one quarter of a given shape including those divided

Operations, relationships....
A use the knowledge that subtraction is the inverse of addition, e.g.
- begin to understand subtraction as 'difference'
- given 14, 6 and 8, make related number sentences 6 + 8 = 14, 14 - 8 = 6, 8 + 6 = 14, 14 - 6 = 8

B understand halving as a way of 'undoing' doubling and vice versa

Mental methods
A use mental recall of addition and subtraction facts to 10, e.g.
- use addition/subtraction facts to 10 and place value to add or subtract multiples of 10, e.g. know 3 + 7 = 10 and use place value to derive 30 + 70 = 100.

B use mental calculation strategies to solve number problems including those involving money and measures, e.g.
- recall doubles to 10 + 10 and other significant doubles, e.g. double 50p is 100p or £1
- use knowledge of doubles to 10 + 10 to derive corresponding halves

Solving numerical problems
A choose the appropriate operation when solving addition and subtraction problems
- use repeated addition to solve multiplication problems
- begin to use repeated subtraction or sharing equally to solve division problems

B solve number problems involving money and measures, e.g.
- add/subtract two-digit and one digit numbers, bridging tens where necessary in contexts using units such as pence, pounds, centimetres

Written methods
A record their work in writing, e.g.
- record their mental calculations as number sentences

Mathematics Attainment Target 3 (MA 3) Shape, Space and Measures

Level 4 (L4)

Properties of shape
A use the properties of 2-D and 3-D shapes, e.g.
- *recognise and name most quadrilaterals, e.g. trapezium, parallelogram, rhombus*
- *recognise right-angled, equilateral, isosceles and scalene triangles*
- *recognise an oblique line of symmetry in a shape*
- *use mathematical terms such as horizontal, vertical, congruent (same size, same shape)*
- *understand properties of shapes, e.g. why a square is a special rectangle*
- *visualise shapes and recognise them in different orientations*

B make 3-D models by linking given faces or edges

Properties of position and movement
A draw common 2-D shapes in different orientations on grids, e.g.
- *complete a rectangle which has two sides drawn at an oblique angle to the grid*

B reflect simple shapes in a mirror line, e.g.
- *use a grid to plot the reflection in a mirror line presented at 45° where the shape touches the line or not*
- *begin to use the distance of vertices from the mirror line to reflect shapes more accurately*

C begin to rotate a simple shape or object about its centre or a vertex

D translate shapes horizontally or vertically

Measures
A choose and use appropriate units and instruments

B interpret, with appropriate accuracy, numbers on a range of measuring instruments, e.g.
- *measure a length using mm, to within 2 mm*
- *measure and drawn acute and obtuse angles to the nearest 5°, when one edge is horizontal/vertical*

C find perimeters of simple shapes and find areas by counting squares, e.g.
- *use the terms 'area' and 'perimeter' accurately and consistently*
- *find areas by counting squares and part squares*
- *begin to find the area of shapes that need to be divided into rectangles*
- *use 'number of squares in a row times number of rows' to find the area of a rectangle*

D use units of time, e.g.
- *calculate time durations that go over the hour*
- *read and interpret timetables*

Level 3 (L3)

Properties of shape
A classify 3-D and 2-D shapes in various ways using mathematical properties such as reflective symmetry for 2-D shapes, e.g.
- *sort objects and shapes using more than one criterion, e.g. pentagon, not pentagon and all edges the same length/not the same length*
- *sort the shapes which have all edges the same length and all angles the same size from a set of mixed shapes and begin to understand the terms 'regular' and 'irregular'*
- *recognise right angles in shapes in different orientations*
- *recognise angles which are bigger/smaller than 90° and begin to know the terms 'obtuse' and 'acute'*
- *recognise right-angled and equilateral triangles*
- *demonstrate that a shape has reflection symmetry by folding and recognise when a shape does not have a line of symmetry*
- *recognise common 3-D shapes, e.g. triangular prism, square-based pyramid*
- *relate 3-D shapes to drawings and photographs of them, including from different viewpoints*

B begin to recognise nets of familiar 3-D shapes, e.g. cube, cuboid, triangular prism, square-based pyramid

Properties of position and movement
A recognise shapes in different orientations

B reflect shapes, presented on a grid, in a vertical or horizontal mirror line, e.g.
- *reflect a shape even if the shape is at 45° to the mirror line, touching the line or not*
- *begin to reflect simple shapes in a mirror line presented at 45°*

C describe position and movement, e.g.
- *use terms such as left/right, clockwise/anticlockwise, quarter turn/90° to give directions along a route*

Measures
A use non-standard units and standard metric units of length, capacity and mass in a range of contexts, e.g.
- *measure a length to the nearest 1/2 cm*
- *read simple scales, e.g. increments of 2, 5 or 10*

B use standard units of time, e.g.
- *read a 12-hour clock and generally calculate time durations that do not go over the hour*

C use a wider range of measures, e.g.
- *begin to understand area as a measure of surface and perimeter as a measure of length*
- *begin to find areas of shapes by counting squares even if not using standard units such as cm² or m²*
- *recognise angles as a measure of turn and know that one whole turn is 360 degrees*

Level 2 (L2)

Properties of shape
A use mathematical names for common 3-D and 2-D shapes, e.g.
- *identify 2-D and 3-D shapes from pictures of them in different orientations, e.g. square, triangle, hexagon, pentagon, octagon, cube, cylinder, sphere, cuboid, pyramid*

B describe their properties, including numbers of sides and corners, e.g.
- *make and talk about shapes referring to features and properties using the language such as edge, face, corner*
- *sort 2-D and 3-D shapes according to a single criterion, e.g. shapes that are pentagons or shapes with a right angle*
- *visualise frequently used 2-D and 3-D shapes*
- *begin to understand the difference between shapes with two dimensions and those with three*
- *recognise the properties that are the same even when a shape is enlarged, e.g. when comparing squares, circles, similar triangles, cubes or spheres of different sizes*

Properties of position and movement
A describe the position of objects, e.g.
- *use ordinal numbers (first, second, third…) to describe the position of objects in a row or when giving directions*
- *recognise and explain that a shape stays the same even when it is held up in different orientations*

B distinguish between straight and turning movements
- *distinguish between left and right and between clockwise and anticlockwise and use these when giving directions*
- *instruct a programmable robot, combining straight-line movements and turns, to move along a defined path or reach a target destination*

C recognise right angles in turns

Measures
A understand angle as a measurement of turn
- *make whole turns, half turns and quarter turns*

B begin to use everyday non-standard and standard units to measure length and mass
- *begin to understand that numbers can be used not only to count discrete objects but also to describe continuous measures, e.g. length*
- *know which measuring tools to use to find, for example, how much an object weighs, how tall a child is, how long it takes to run around the edge of the playground, how much water it takes to fill the water tray*
- *read scales to the nearest labelled division - begin to make sensible estimates in relation to familiar units*

C begin to use a wider range of measures
- *make and use a 'right angle checker'*
- *use a time line to order daily events and ordinal numbers (first, second, third…) to describe the order of some regular events*

Mathematics Attainment Target 4 (MA 4) Handling Data

Level 4 (L4)

Processing and representing data

A collect discrete data, e.g.
- given a problem, suggest possible answers and data to collect
- test a hypothesis about the frequency of an event by collecting data, e.g. collect dice scores to test ideas about how many scores of 6 will occur during 50 throws of a dice

B group data, where appropriate, in equal class intervals, e.g.
- decide on a suitable class interval when collecting or representing data about pupils' hours per week spent watching TV

C record discrete data using a frequency table

D represent collected data in frequency diagrams, e.g.
- suggest an appropriate frequency diagram to represent particular data, e.g. decide whether a bar chart, Venn diagram or pictogram would be most appropriate and for pictograms use one symbol to represent, say, 2, 5, 10 or 100

E construct simple line graphs
- decide upon an appropriate scale for a graph, e.g. labelled divisions representing 2, 5, 10, 100

F continue to use Venn and Carroll diagrams to record their sorting and classifying of information, e.g.
- represent sorting using two criteria typical of level 3 and 4 mathematics such as sorting numbers using properties 'multiples of 8' and 'multiples of 6'

Interpreting data

A understand and use the mode and range to describe sets of data
- use mode and range to describe data relating to shoe sizes in their class and begin to compare their data with data from another class

B interpret frequency diagrams and simple line graphs
- interpret simple pie charts
- interpret the scale on bar graphs and line graphs, reading between the labelled divisions, e.g. reading 17 on a scale labelled in fives
- interpret the total amount of data represented
- compare data sets and respond to questions, e.g. 'How does our data about favourite TV programmes compare to the data from Year 3 children?'
- in the context of data relating to everyday situations, understand the language of probability such as 'more likely, equally likely, fair, unfair, certain'

Level 3 (L3)

Processing and representing data

A gather information, e.g.
- decide what data to collect to answer a question, e.g. what is the most common way to travel to school
- make appropriate choices for recording data, e.g. a tally chart or frequency table

B construct bar charts and pictograms, where the symbol represents a group of units, e.g.
- decide how best to represent data, e.g. whether a bar chart, Venn diagram or pictogram would show the information most clearly
- decide upon an appropriate scale for a graph, e.g. labelled divisions of 2, or, for a pictogram, one symbol to represent 2 or 5

C use Venn and Carroll diagrams to record their sorting and classifying of information, e.g.
- represent sorting using one or two criteria typical of level 2 and 3 mathematics, e.g. shapes sorted using properties such as right angles and equal sides

Interpreting data

A extract and interpret information presented in simple tables, lists, bar charts and pictograms, e.g.
- use a key to interpret represented data
- read scales labelled in twos, fives and tens, including reading between labelled divisions such as a point halfway between 40 and 50 or 8 and 10
- compare data, e.g. say how many more... than... and recognise the category that has most/least
- respond to questions of a more complex nature such as 'How many children took part in this survey altogether?' or 'How would the data differ if we asked the children in Year 6?'
- in the context of data relating to everyday situations, understand the idea of 'certain' and 'impossible' relating to probability

Level 2 (L2)

Processing and representing data

A sort objects and classify them using more than one criterion, e.g.
- sort a given set of shapes using two criteria such as triangle/not triangle and blue/not blue

B understand vocabulary relating to handling data, e.g.
- understand vocabulary such as sort, group, set, list, table, most common, most popular

C collect and sort data to test a simple hypothesis, e.g.
- count a show of hands to test the hypothesis 'most children in our class are in bed by 7:30pm'

D record results in simple lists, tables, pictograms and block graphs, e.g.
- present information in lists, tables and simple graphs where one symbol or block represents one unit
- enter data into a simple computer database

Interpreting data

A communicate their findings, using the simple lists, tables, pictograms and block graphs they have recorded, e.g.
- respond to questions about the data they have presented, e.g. how many of our names have 5 letters?
- pose similar questions about their data for others to answer

Assessing Pupil Progress in Mathematics (APP)
and Identifying Gaps in Pupil's Learning (Year 4 - Level 2)

Name		Date	

This test can be used to confirm a teacher's informal assessment of a pupil. It can also be used to indicate gaps in a pupil's learning.

How to confirm a teacher's informal assessment of a pupil

The test is in two parts. One part consists of an un-timed written paper test for the pupil to complete unaided. The other part (found below) consists of a simple grid for the teacher to complete after observing the pupil in a normal classroom situation. This part of the assessment indicates performance mainly against Attainment Target 1 – Using and Applying Mathematics. The scores for the two tests should be added together and a National Curriculum sub-level awarded using the information in the table at the bottom of this page. The resulting score should give a clear indication of which sub-level the pupil is working at within the levels found in the English National Curriculum.

How to indicate gaps in a pupil's learning.

Each question on the written paper is accompanied by the learning objective it represents taken from the tables reproduced at the beginning of the book. By referring to the incorrect questions a list of learning objectives which indicate the gaps in the pupil's learning can quickly and easily be made up.

Teacher Assessment of Attainment Target 1 – Using & Applying (Ma1)	Mark
2 marks indicates competent 1 mark indicates some ability 0 mark indicates unable to carry out	0,1 or 2 for each statement
Ma1/L2 – Problem solving - Part A Select the mathematics they use in some classroom activities with support	
Ma1/L2 – Communicating - Part A Discuss their work using mathematical language	
Ma1/L2 – Communicating - Part B Begin to represent their work using symbols and simple diagrams	
Ma1/L2 – Reasoning - Part A Explain why an answer is correct	
Ma1/L2 – Reasoning - Part B Predict what comes next in a simple pattern and give reasons for opinion	
Total =	

	Actual	Possible
Teacher Assessment of AT1 from above.		10
Paper Test Score		40
Total		50
Sub Level Awarded		

Level 2a high	**= 42 - 50**
Level 2b secure	**= 32 - 41**
Level 2c low	**= 21 - 31**
Below Level 2	**= 20 or less**

. How many cherries are there?

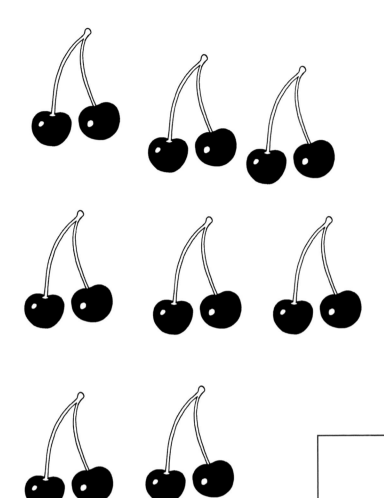

cherries

Teacher's notes

Ma2/L2
Numbers and the number system
Part A

Count sets of objects reliably

1 mark

2. Put these numbers in order, smallest first.

45   69   71   92   29

Ma2/L2
Numbers and the number system
Part B

Begin to understand the place value of each digit; use this to order numbers up to 100

1 mark

3. Write the next two numbers in this sequence.

3	6	9		

Teacher's no

Ma2/L2
Numbers and the
number system
Part C

Recognise sequen
of numbers, includ
odd and even
numbers

1 mark

4. Write the next two numbers in this sequence.

20	40	60		

Ma2/L2
Numbers and the
number system
Part C

Recognise sequenc
of numbers, includin
odd and even
numbers

1 mark

5. Tick the boxes that have an odd number inside.

24	12	28	13	14

45	7	83	4	67

Ma2/L2
Numbers and the
number system
Part C

Recognise sequence
of numbers, including
odd and even
numbers

1 mark

. If Jenny ate half of the grapes – how many did she eat?

	grapes

Ma2/L2
Fractions
Part A

Begin to use halves and quarters

1 mark

. If Felix ate a quarter of the grapes – how many did he eat?

	grapes

Ma2/L2
Fractions
Part A

Begin to use halves and quarters

1 mark

. What is half of 28?

Ma2/L2
Fractions
Part A

Begin to use halves and quarters

1 mark

. What is half of 16?

Ma2/L2
Fractions
Part A

Begin to use halves and quarters

1 mark

10. Colour in a half of this shape.

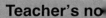

Teacher's no

Ma2/L2
Fractions
Part B

Relate the concep
half of a small qua
to the concept of h
of a shape

1 mark

11. Colour in a quarter of this shape.

Ma2/L2
Fractions
Part B

Relate the concep
half of a small qua
to the concept of h
of a shape

1 mark

12. Find the difference between 17 and 5.

Ma2/L2
Operations,
relationships
between them
Part A

Use the knowledge
that subtraction is
inverse of addition

1 mark

13. Use 5 + 8 = 13 to make two different
take away sentences.

So 13 – ☐ = ☐

and 13 – ☐ = ☐

Ma2/L2
Operations,
relationships
between them
Part A

Use the knowledge
that subtraction is
inverse of addition

2 marks

4. If I double a number, the answer is 16.

   What number did I double?

Ma2/L2
Operations, relationships between them Part B

Understand halving as a way of 'undoing' doubling and vice versa

1 mark

---

15. If I halve a number, the answer is 9.

    What number did I half?

Ma2/L2
Operations, relationships between them Part B

Understand halving as a way of 'undoing' doubling and vice versa

1 mark

16.

   $4 +$ $= 10$

Ma2/L2
Mental Methods Part A

Use mental recall of addition and subtraction facts to 10

1 mark

17.

   $3 + 4 = 7$

   so $30 + 40 =$

Ma2/L2
Mental Methods Part A

Use mental recall of addition and subtraction facts to 10

1 mark

18. How much money is here:

20p 20p 20p 5p

[ ] p

19. A pencil measures 11cm and
another pencil measures 11cm.
If you put them in a line how
much will they measure altogether?

[ ] cm

20. Harriet has 14p,
Eleanor has 15p,
and Charlie has 16p.

How much do they have altogether?

[ ] p

21. There were 100 books, but 7 books
went missing.

How many are there now?

[ ]

22. What is 9p add 6p add 5p?

p

Ma2/L2
Solving Number Problems
Part B

Solve number problems involving money and measures

1 mark

23. What is 52p take away 7p?

p

Ma2/L2
Solving Number Problems
Part B

Solve number problems involving money and measures

1 mark

24. There are 9 birds but 3 fly away so there are 6 left.

Ma2/L2
Written methods
Part A

Record their work in writing

1 mark

Choose numbers and symbols to make a number sentence

| 3 | 9 | 6 | = | + | - |

| | | | | |

25. What is this shape? Tick the correct answer.

Pentagon,

Hexagon,

Octagon

Teacher's no

Ma3/L2
Properties of Sha
Part A

Use mathematical names for commor 3-D and 2-D shape

1 mark

---

26. Tick the two octagons.

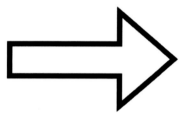

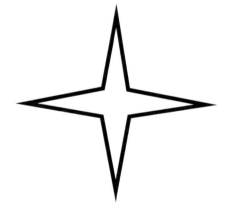

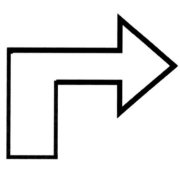

Ma3/L2
Properties of Shap
Part B

Describe their properties, including number of sides anc corners

1 mark

27. Write the number of corners next to the name of the shape.

Shape	Number of corners
Cube	
Cone	
Sphere	

Teacher's notes

Ma3/L2
Properties of Shape Part B

Describe their properties, including number of sides and corners

1 mark

28. Draw an arrow to show whether the shape is 2-D or 3-D.

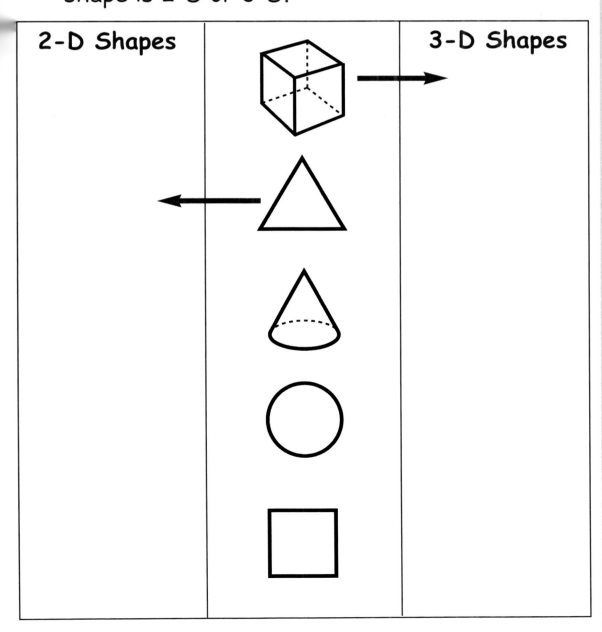

2-D Shapes		3-D Shapes

Ma3/L2
Properties of Shape Part B

Describe their properties, including number of sides and corners

1 mark

29. What is the name of the third shape?

It is a...

Ma3/L2
Properties of
position and
movement
Part A

Describe the positi
of objects

1 mark

---

30. Here is an arrow. Draw another arrow on the
left hand side of it.

Ma3/L2
Properties of
position and
movement
Part B

Distinguish between
straight and turning
movements

1 mark

---

31. If I face South and turn one right angle
clockwise – where am I facing now?

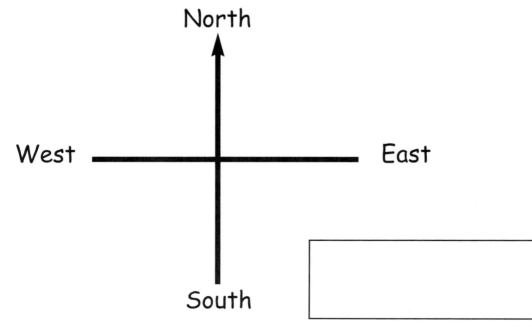

Ma3/L2
Properties of
position and
movement
Part C

Recognise right angle
in turns

1 mark

© **Topical Resources.** May be photocopied for classroom use only.

32. Tick the shape that has made a half turn.

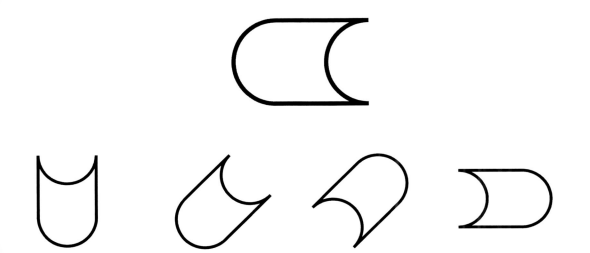

Teacher's notes

Ma3/L2
Measures
Part A

Understand angle as a measurement of turn – make whole turns, half turns and quarter turns.

1 mark

33. What would you use to measure the following? Show with arrows.

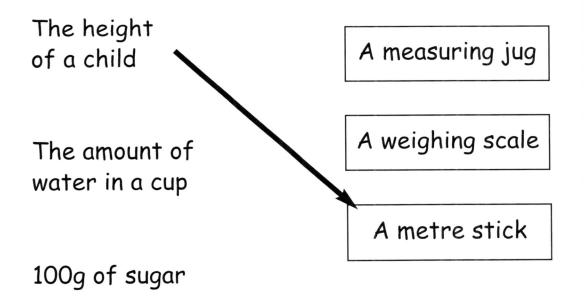

The height of a child

A measuring jug

The amount of water in a cup

A weighing scale

A metre stick

100g of sugar

34. Put these days in order, the 1st one has been done for you.

Friday

~~Monday~~

Wednesday

Saturday

Thursday

Tuesday

1st	Monday
2nd	
3rd	
4th	
5th	
6th	

35. Look at the Carroll diagram. How many more blue triangles are there than red triangles?

	Triangle	Not Triangle
Blue	7	56
Not Blue	4	35

Graph to show the favourite subject of children in Class 1

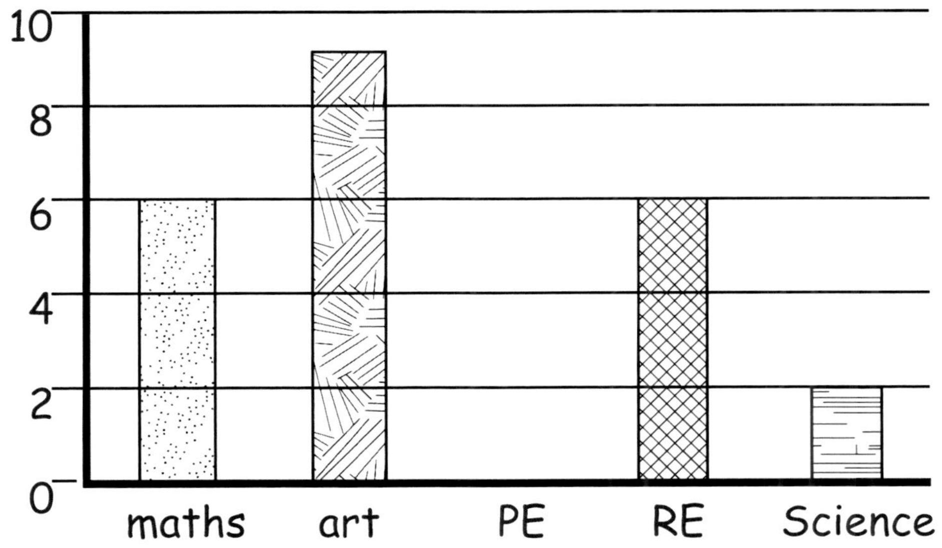

36. Which is the most popular subject?

Ma4/L2
Processing and representing data
Part B

Understand vocabulary relating to handling data

1 mark

37. The graph is not finished.
Here is how many people liked PE.

|||| || How many is this?

Ma4/L2
Processing and representing data
Part C

Collect and sort data to test a simple hypothesis

1 mark

38. Draw the amount of children who liked PE on the graph above.

Ma4/L2
Processing and representing data
Part D

Record results in simple lists, tables, pictograms and block graphs

1 mark

39. How many children like maths best?

Ma4/L2
Interpreting data
Part A

Communicate their findings, using the simple lists, tables, pictograms and block graphs they have recorded

1 mark

Assessing Pupil Progress in Mathematics (APP)
and Identifying Gaps in Pupil's Learning (Year 4 - Level 3)

Name		Date	

This test can be used to confirm a teacher's informal assessment of a pupil. It can also be used to indicate gaps in a pupil's learning.

How to confirm a teacher's informal assessment of a pupil

The test is in two parts. One part consists of an un-timed written paper test for the pupil to complete unaided. The other part (found below) consists of a simple grid for the teacher to complete after observing the pupil in a normal classroom situation. This part of the assessment indicates performance mainly against Attainment Target 1 – Using and Applying Mathematics. The scores for the two tests should be added together and a National Curriculum sub-level awarded using the information in the table at the bottom of this page. The resulting score should give a clear indication of which sub-level the pupil is working at within the levels found in the English National Curriculum.

How to indicate gaps in a pupil's learning.

Each question on the written paper is accompanied by the learning objective it represents taken from the tables reproduced at the beginning of the book. By referring to the incorrect questions a list of learning objectives which indicate the gaps in the pupil's learning can quickly and easily be made up.

Teacher Assessment of Attainment Target 1 – Using & Applying (Ma1) and some of Attainment Target 4 – Handling and Data (Ma4) 1 mark indicates some ability 0 mark indicates unable to carry out	Mark 0 or 1 for each statement
Ma1/L3 – Problem solving - Part A Select the mathematics they use in a wider range of classroom activities	
Ma1/L3 – Problem solving - Part B Try different approaches	
Ma1/L3 – Problem solving - Part B Find ways of overcoming difficulties that arise when they are solving problems	
Ma1/L3 – Communicating - Part A Begin to organise their work and check results	
Ma1/L3 – Communicating - Part B Discuss their mathematical work and begin to explain	
Ma1/L3 – Communicating - Part C Use and interpret mathematics symbols and diagram	
Ma1/L3 – Reasoning - Part A Understand a general statement by finding particular examples that match it	
Ma1/L3 – Reasoning - Part B Review their work and reasoning	
Ma 4/L3 – Processing and representing data – Part A Gather information	
Ma 4/L3 – Processing and representing data – Part B Construct bar charts and pictograms, where the symbol represents a group of units	
Total =	

	Actual	Possible		
Teacher Assessment of AT1 from above.		10	**Level 3a high**	**= 42 - 50**
Paper Test Score		40	**Level 3b secure**	**= 32 - 41**
Total		50	**Level 3c low**	**= 21 - 31**
Sub Level Awarded			**Below Level 3**	**= 20 or less**

. Put these numbers in order – smallest first.

| 872 | 38 | 299 | 82 | 897 |

| | | | | |

Teacher's notes

Ma2/L3
Numbers and the
number system
Part A

Understand place
value in numbers to
1000

1 mark

2. Round these numbers to the nearest 100.

The nearest 100 to 266 is

The nearest 100 to 246 is

Ma2/L3
Numbers and the
number system
Part B

Use place value to
make approximations

1 mark

3. Tick the coldest place.

Glasgow -6°C

Preston 9°C

London 17°C

Belfast -4°C

Scotland

Ireland

England

Wales

Ma2/L3
Numbers and the
number system
Part C

Recognise negative
numbers in contexts
such as temperature

1 mark

4. What is the difference in temperature between Preston and Glasgow?

°C

Ma2/L3
Numbers and the
number system
Part C

Recognise negative
numbers in contexts
such as temperature

1 mark

5. Write in the missing numbers:

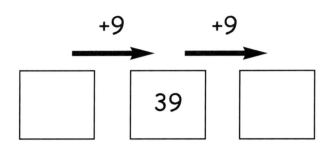

+9   +9

[   ] | 39 | [   ]

Ma2/L3
Numbers and the
number system
Part D

Recognise a wider
range of sequence.

1 mark [   ]

6. Write in the next number in the sequence.

| 35 | | 45 | | 55 | | [   ] | | 75 |

Ma2/L3
Numbers and the
number system
Part D

Recognise a wider
range of sequences

1 mark [   ]

7. Sally has a bunch of 33 grapes. She eats $\frac{1}{3}$.
How many grapes Sally eat?

[grapes]

Ma2/L3
Fractions and
decimals
Part A

Use simple fractions
that are several parts
of a whole and
recognise when two
simple fractions are
equivalent

1 mark [   ]

8. Circle the fractions that are equal to $\frac{1}{2}$.

$\frac{4}{8}$ $\frac{3}{4}$ $\frac{2}{4}$ $\frac{2}{1}$

Ma2/L3
Fractions and
decimals
Part A

Use simple fractions
that are several parts
of a whole and
recognise when two
simple fractions are
equivalent

1 mark [   ]

9. Emily buys a pen for 45p and a ruler for 59p.
    How much does she spend altogether?

    [ ]

Teacher's notes

Ma2/L3
Fractions and decimals
Part B

Begin to use decimal notation in contexts such as money

1 mark [ ]

10.

$$15 \times 5 = 75$$

$$\text{so } 75 \div 5 = \quad [\quad]$$

Ma2/L3
Operations, relationships between them
Part A

Derive associated division facts from known multiplication facts

1 mark [ ]

11.

$$7 + 4 = 6 + \quad [\quad]$$

Ma2/L3
Operations, relationships between them
Part B

Begin to understand the role of '=', the 'equals' sign

1 mark [ ]

12.

$$21 + 23 = \quad [\quad]$$

Ma2/L3
Mental Methods
Part A

Add and Subtract two-digit numbers mentally

1 mark [ ]

13.

$$56 - 49 = \quad [\quad]$$

Ma2/L3
Mental Methods
Part A

Add and Subtract two-digit numbers mentally

1 mark [ ]

14.

$$\boxed{} \times \boxed{} = 30$$

$$\boxed{} \times \boxed{} = 14$$

Teacher's not

Ma2/L3
Mental Methods
Part B

*Use mental recall
the 2, 3, 4, 5 and 1
multiplication table*

2 marks

---

15. Mary has 40p. She spends $\frac{1}{4}$.
How much does she spend?

$$\boxed{} \text{ p}$$

Ma2/L3
Mental Methods
Part B

*Use mental recall o
the 2, 3, 4, 5 and 1(
multiplication tables*

1 mark

---

16. Chloe has £2. She buys a book for 75p.
How much does she have left?

$$\text{£} \boxed{}$$

Ma2/L3
Solving numerical
problems
Part A

*Use mental recall of
addition and
subtraction facts to 2
in solving problems
involving larger
numbers*

1 mark

---

17. Owen has more than 10 sweets but fewer
than 20 sweets. When he shared them equally
between himself and 2 friends he had none
left over.

How many sweets could he have?

$$\boxed{} \text{ sweets}$$

Ma2/L3
Solving numerical
problems
Part B

*Solve whole number
problems including
those involving
multiplication or
division that may give
rise to remainders*

1 mark

18. There are 75 children for dinner.
Five children sit at each table.

How many tables are needed?

19.

808 + 101 =

20.

135 - 73 =

21.

What is 85 x 4 =

22. Tick the divisions that have an answer of 3.

30 ÷ 10 =	30 ÷ 3 =
20 ÷ 4 =	9 ÷ 3 =

Teacher's not

Ma2/L3
Written Methods
Part B

*Multiply and divide
two-digit numbers
2, 3, 4 and 5 as we
as 10 with whole
number answers a
remainders*

1 mark

23. Tick the divisions that have a remainder of 3.

12 ÷ 5 =	18 ÷ 5 =
23 ÷ 5 =	27 ÷ 5 =

Ma2/L3
Written Methods
Part B

*Multiply and divide
two-digit numbers by
2, 3, 4 and 5 as well
as 10 with whole
number answers and
remainders*

1 mark

24. Write the number of right-angles in each shape.

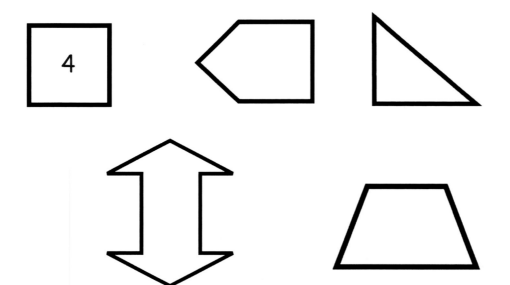

Ma3/L3
Properties of shape
Part A

*Classify 3-D and 2-D
shapes in various
ways using
mathematical
properties such as
reflective symmetry fo
2-D shapes*

1 mark

25a. Put a tick in the right-angle triangle.

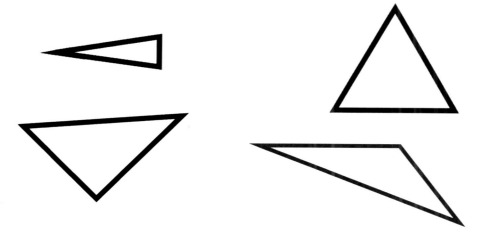

25b. Put a circle around the equilateral triangle.

26. Tick the square-based pyramid.

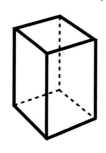

Ma3/L3
Properties of shape
Part A

Classify 3-D and 2-D shapes in various ways using mathematical properties such as reflective symmetry for 2-D shapes

2 marks

Ma3/L3
Properties of shape
Part A

Classify 3-D and 2-D shapes in various ways using mathematical properties such as reflective symmetry for 2-D shapes

1 mark

27. Put a cross on the nets which will **not** make a cube.

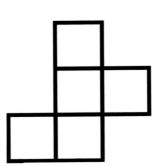

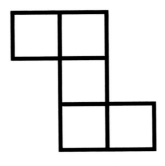

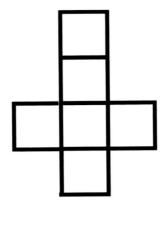

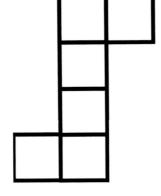

Teacher's not

Ma3/L3
Properties of sha
Part B

Begin to recognise nets of familiar 3-D shapes

1 mark

28. What is the name of this shape?

It is a...

Teacher's notes

Ma3/L3
Properties of position and movement
Part A

Recognise shapes in different orientations

1 mark

29. Reflect the shaded shapes in the mirror line.

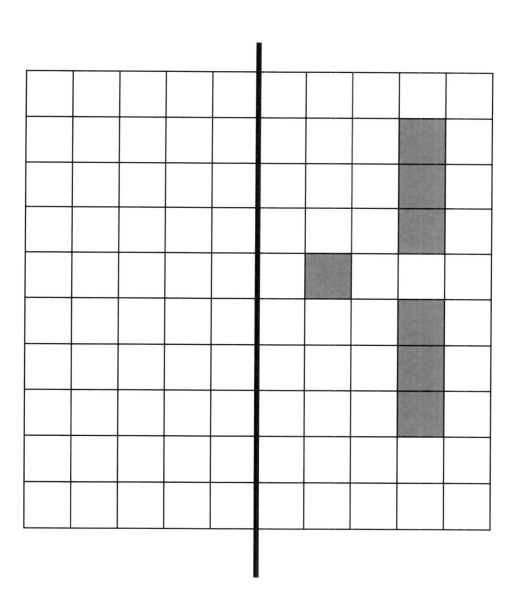

Ma3/L3
Properties of position and movement
Part B

Reflect shapes presented on a grid, in a vertical or horizontal mirror line

1 mark

30. Tick the correct word.

start   finish

The shape above has been rotated 90°.
Which way has it been rotated?

clockwise ☐   anticlockwise ☐

Teacher's not

Ma3/L3
Properties of
position and
movement
Part C

Describe position a
movement

1 mark ☐

---

31. How long is this line?   cm

Ma3/L3
Measures
Part A

Use non-standard
units and standard
metric units of lengt
capacity and mass
range of contexts

1 mark ☐

---

32. How long is a lesson that starts at
9.10am and finishes at 9.50am?

minutes

Ma3/L3
Measures
Part B

Use standard units c
time

1 mark ☐

---

33. How many degrees make a whole turn?

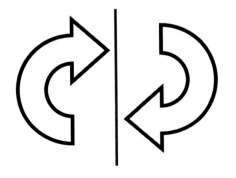

o

Ma3/L3
Measures
Part C

Use a wider range of
measures

1 mark ☐

34. Sarah is 13 years old and her birthday is in April. Amy is 4 years younger than Sarah and her birthday is in January. Put Amy and Sarah on the Carroll Diagram.

	January to June	July to December
13 years old		
9 years old		

Teacher's notes

Ma4/L3
Processing and representing data
Parts A and B

(See Teacher Assessment on the first page of this test paper.)

Ma4/L3
Processing and representing data
Part C

Use Venn and Carroll diagrams to record their sorting and classifying of information

2 marks

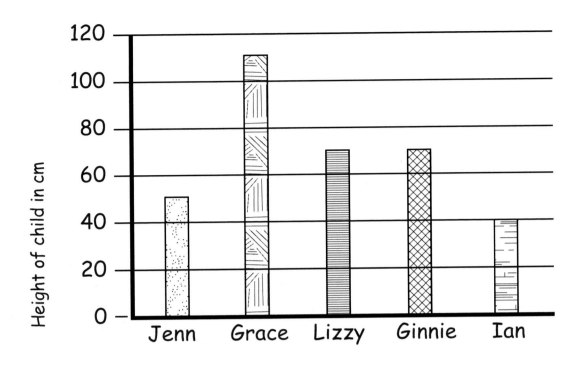

Graph to show the height of 5 toddlers

Height of child in cm

35. How tall is Grace?

cm

36. How much taller is Grace than Ian?

cm

37. What is the total height of Ian and Ginnie?

cm

Teacher's not

Ma4/L3
Interpreting data
Part A

*Extract and interpret
information presente
in simple tables, lists
bar charts and
pictograms*

3 marks

Assessing Pupil Progress in Mathematics (APP)
and Identifying Gaps in Pupil's Learning (Year 4 - Level 4)

Name		Date	

This test can be used to confirm a teacher's informal assessment of a pupil. It can also be used to indicate gaps in a pupil's learning.

How to confirm a teacher's informal assessment of a pupil

The test is in two parts. One part consists of an un-timed written paper test for the pupil to complete unaided. The other part (found below) consists of a simple grid for the teacher to complete after observing the pupil in a normal classroom situation. This part of the assessment indicates performance mainly against Attainment Target 1 – Using and Applying Mathematics. The scores for the two tests should be added together and a National Curriculum sub-level awarded using the information in the table at the bottom of this page. The resulting score should give a clear indication of which sub-level the pupil is working at within the levels found in the English National Curriculum.

How to indicate gaps in a pupil's learning.

Each question on the written paper is accompanied by the learning objective it represents taken from the tables reproduced at the beginning of the book. By referring to the incorrect questions a list of learning objectives which indicate the gaps in the pupil's learning can quickly and easily be made up.

Teacher Assessment of Attainment Target 1 – Using & Applying (Ma1) and some of Attainment Target 4 – Handling and Data (Ma4) 2 marks indicates competent 1 mark indicates some ability 0 mark indicates unable to carry out	Mark 0,1 or 2 for each statement
Ma1/L4 – Problem solving - Part A Develop own strategies for solving problems	
Ma1/L4 – Problem solving - Part B Use their own strategies within mathematics and in applying mathematics to practical context	
Ma1/L4 – Communicating - Part A Show understanding of situations by describing them mathematically using symbols, words and diagrams	
Ma1/L4 – Reasoning - Part A Search for a solution by trying out ideas of their own	
Ma4/L4 – Processing and representing data -Parts A-D	
Total =	

	Actual	Possible
Teacher Assessment of AT1 from above.		10
Paper Test Score		40
Total		50
Sub Level Awarded		

Level 4a high	**= 42 - 50**
Level 4b secure	**= 32 - 41**
Level 4c low	**= 21 - 31**
Below Level 4	**= 20 or less**

1. Fill in the missing numbers in this sequence.

| | 2.7 | 2.8 | | | 3.1 | |

Ma2/L4
Numbers and the
number system
Part A

Recognise and
describe number
patterns

1 mark

2. Tick the boxes that are multiples of 4.

| 25 | 52 | 12 | 15 | 20 |

Ma2/L4
Numbers and the
number system
Part B

Recognise and des
number relationship
including multiple, f
and square

1 mark

3.

$160 \times 10 =$

$359 \times 100 =$

$180 \div 10 =$

$4500 \div 100 =$

Ma2/L4
Numbers and the
number system
Part C

Use place value to
multiply and divide
whole numbers by
or 100

2 marks

4. How many minutes are there in $\frac{3}{4}$ of an hour?

minutes

Ma2/L4
Fractions, decimals
percentages and
ratio
Part A

Recognise
approximate
proportions of a
whole and use
simple fractions and
percentages to
describe these

1 mark

5. Put these numbers in order – smallest first.

| 3.04 | 0.4 | 0.24 | 4 |

| | | | |

Ma2/L4
Fractions, decimals, percentages and ratio
Part B

Order decimals to three decimal places

1 mark

6. To make a Smoothie, for every three apples you use one pineapple. If you use 12 apples, how many pineapples will you need?

pineapples

Ma2/L4
Fractions, decimals, percentages and ratio
Part C

Begin to understand simple ratio

1 mark

7. I am thinking of a number.
I take away 2, then I halve the number.
The answer is 6.
What number am I thinking of?

Ma2/L4
Operations, relationships between them
Part A

Use inverse operations

1 mark

8.

$24 = \boxed{} \div 4$

Ma2/L4
Operations, relationships between them
Part A

Use inverse operations

1 mark

9. Write a digit in each box to make this multiplication sentence correct.

$$\boxed{2}\,\boxed{} \times \boxed{4} = \boxed{}\,\boxed{4}$$

Teacher's note

Ma2/L4
Operations, relationships between them
Part A

Use inverse operations

1 mark

10. Write a number in the box to make the sum balance.

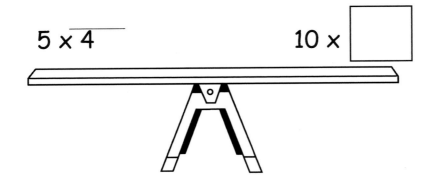

5×4 $10 \times \boxed{}$

Ma2/L4
Operations, relationships between them
Part A

Use inverse operations

1 mark

11.

$$16 - (3 + 1) = \boxed{}$$

Ma2/L4
Operations, relationships between them
Part B

Understand the use brackets in simple calculations

1 mark

12.

$$24 \div 6 = \boxed{}$$

Ma2/L4
Operations, relationships between them
Part C

Quickly derive divisic facts that correspond to multiplication facts up to 10 x 10

1 mark

3.

$$350 + \boxed{} = 1000$$

Ma2/L4
Mental methods
Part A

Use a range of mental methods of computation with the four operations

1 mark

14.

8 x 5 =	6 x 8 =	4 x 6 =
40 ÷ 8 =	48 ÷ 6 =	24 ÷ 6 =
4 x 7 =	4 x 8 =	3 x 7 =
28 ÷ 7 =	32 ÷ 4 =	21 ÷ 3 =

Ma2/L4
Mental methods
Part B

Recall multiplication facts up to 10 x 10 and quickly derive corresponding division facts

1 mark

15. There are 33 children in Mrs. Newton's class.
There is one more boy than girl.
How many girls are there in the class?

girls

Ma2/L4
Solving numerical problems
Part A

Solve problems with or without a calculator

1 mark

16. Michaela buys 4 pens at 96p.
How much do they cost altogether?

£

Ma2/L4
Solving numerical problems
Part B

Check the reasonableness of results with reference to the context or size of numbers

1 mark

17. In the Blair family, to find the amount of pocket money...

Multiply their age by 4p, then add 9p.

How much will a 6 year old get? ☐ p

Teacher's no

Ma2/L4
Solving numerica
problems
Part C

*Begin to use simp
formulae expresse
words*

1 mark ☐

18.

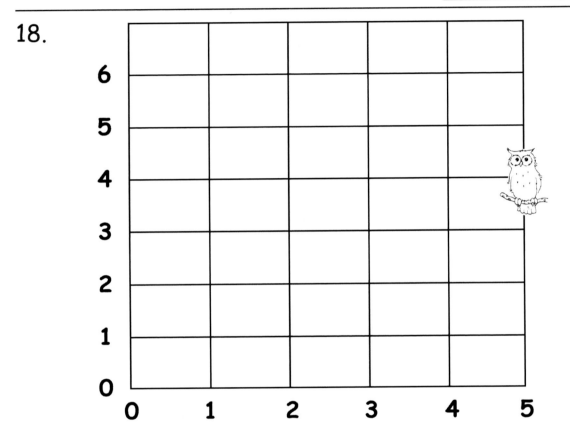

What are the co-ordinates of the owl?

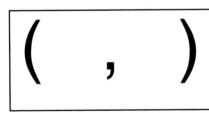

(,)

Ma2/L4
Solving numerica
problems
Part D

*Use and interpret
co-ordinates in the
quadrant*

1 mark ☐

19.

537 – 86 = ☐

Ma2/L4
Written and
calculator methods
Part A

*Use efficient written
methods of addition,
subtraction and of
short multiplication
and division*

1 mark ☐

20.

$73 \times 80 =$ [____]

Teacher's notes

Ma2/L4
Written and calculator methods Part A

Use efficient written methods of addition, subtraction and of short multiplication and division

1 mark [____]

21. There are 60 pencils. They are stored in pots of 5. How many pots do we need?

[____] pots

5 Pencils

Ma2/L4
Written and calculator methods Part A

Use efficient written methods of addition, subtraction and of short multiplication and division

1 mark [____]

22.

$7.2 + 7.2 =$ [____]

Ma2/L4
Written and calculator methods Part B

Add and subtract decimals to two places

1 mark [____]

23.

$$6.33 - 2.72 = \boxed{}$$

24.

$$2.9 \times 6 = \boxed{}$$

25. Draw in any lines of symmetry on these shapes.

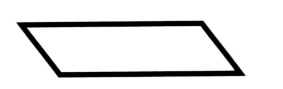
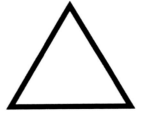
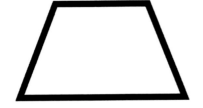

6. Add these two shapes to the net below to make a net for a cuboid.

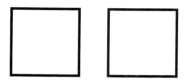

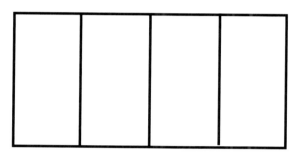

Teacher's notes

Ma3/L4
Properties of shape
Part B

Make 3-D models by linking given faces or edges

1 mark

27. Draw 2 more lines to make a rectangle.

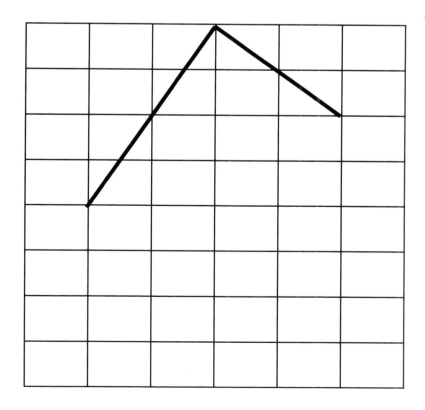

Ma3/L4
Properties of position and movement
Part A

Draw common 2-D shapes in different orientations on grids

1 mark

41

28. Draw in a line of symmetry.

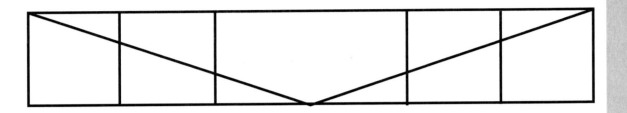

29. Rotate this shape one half turn about its centre 'c' and draw the new shape.

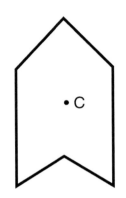

• c

30. Translate this shape 3 squares to the left.

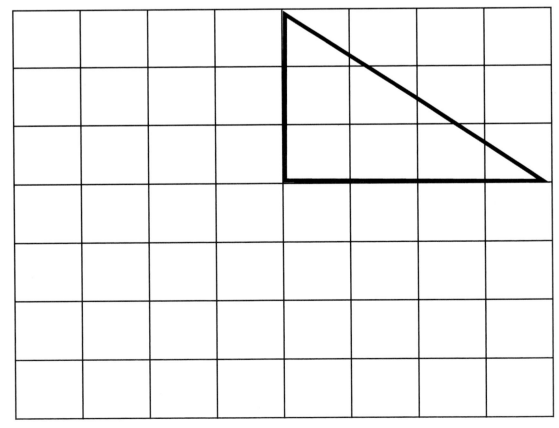

Ma3/L4
Properties of position and movement Part B

*Reflect simple sh.
in a mirror line*

1 mark

Ma3/L4
Properties of position and movement Part C

*Begin to rotate a simple shape or ob
about its centre or vertex*

1 mark

Ma3/L4
Properties of position and movement Part D

Translate shapes horizontally or vertically

1 mark

1. What units would you use to measure the following? Show with arrows.

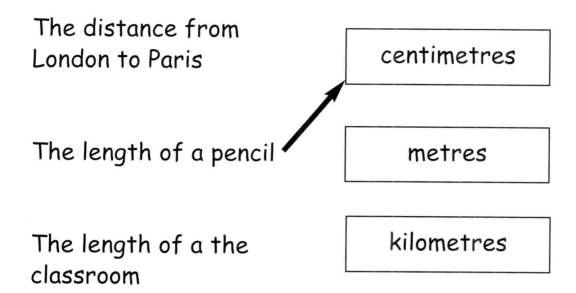

The distance from London to Paris

The length of a pencil

The length of a the classroom

centimetres

metres

kilometres

Teacher's notes

Ma3/L4
Measures
Part A

Choose and use appropriate units and instruments

1 mark

---

32. How many Kilograms does this scale read?

0kg   1kg

kg

Ma3/L4
Measures
Part B

Interpret, with appropriate accuracy, numbers on a range of measuring instruments

1 mark

33. If one side of a square measures 5cm,
    what is the area and perimeter of the shape?

Area = [   ] cm²   Perimeter = [   ] cm

Ma3/L4
Measures
Part C

Find the perimete
simple shapes ar
find areas by cou
squares

1 mark [   ]

---

34. A television programme begins at 5.50pm
    and lasts for 50 minutes.
    At what time does it finish?

[   ] pm

Ma3/L4
Measures
Part D

Use units of time

1 mark [   ]

Graph to show the favourite colours of children in a school

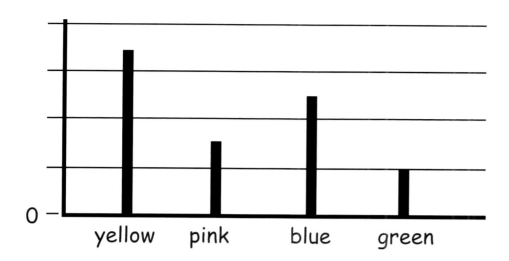

Ma4/L4
Processing and representing data
Parts A, B, C and D

(See Teacher Assessment on the first page of this test paper.)

35. If pink represents 15 pupils, label the scale on the y axis that starts from 0.

Ma4/L4
Processing and representing data
Part E

Construct simple line graphs

1 mark

36. Here is a table to show how many children went to the school library during morning and afternoon breaks each day of a week.

Ma4/L4
Interpreting data
Part B
(note – this statement is slightly out of order)

Interpret frequency diagrams and simple line graphs

1 mark

	Morning break	Afternoon break
Monday	16	35
Tuesday	13	14
Wednesday	32	12
Thursday	23	24
Friday	34	34

On which days were there a total of more than 50 visitors?

and

37 Look at the table below. How many children are 8 years old in class 2?

	Class 1	Class 2
7 years old	9	4
8 years old	7	13
9 years old	10	14

children

Ma4/L4
Processing and representing da
Part F

Continue to use ‘ and Carroll diagra to record their so and classifying o information

1 mark

38. These are the test scores for 7 children.

15   15   11   15   18   12   20

What is the mode?

What is the range?

Ma4/L4
Interpreting data
Part A

Understand and u: the mode and ranç describe sets of d:

2 marks

Answers **Year 4 - Level 2**

1	16 cherries
2	29, 45, 69, 71, 92
3	12, 15
4	80, 100
5	13, 45, 7, 83, 67
6	10 grapes
7	5 grapes
8	14
9	8
10	e.g.
11	e.g.
12	12
13	13 - 8 = 5 13 - 5 = 8
14	8
15	18
16	6
17	70
18	65p
19	22cm
20	45p
21	93
22	20p
23	45p
24	9 - 3 = 6

25   Hexagon

26

27   8, 1, 0

28   *3D Shapes*

       2D Shapes

29   Hexagon

30

31   West

32

33   *The height of a child* ....A metre stick
       The amount of water in a cup....A measuring jug
       100g of sugar....A weighing scale

34   *2nd* Tuesday
       3rd Wednesday
       4th Thursday
       5th Friday
       6th Saturday

35   3

36   Art

37   7

38   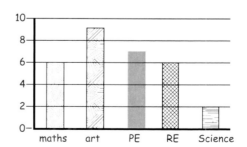

39   6

1   38, 82, 299, 872, 897

2   300, 200

3   Glasgow -6°C

4   15°C

5   30, 48

6   65

7   11 grapes

8    $\frac{4}{8}$ $\frac{2}{4}$

9   £1.04

10   15

11   5

12   44

13   7

14   e.g.   3 x 10 = 30   2 x 7 = 14

15   10p

16   £1.25

17   12 or 15 or 18 sweets

18   15

19   909

20   62

21   340

22   30 ÷ 10 =   9 ÷ 3 =

23   18 ÷ 5 =   23 ÷ 5 =

24
4   3   1

0   0

25a

25b

26

27
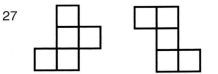

28   hexagon

29
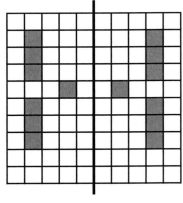

30   clockwise

31   12 cm

32   40 minutes

33   360°

34

	January to June	July to December
13 years old	Sarah	
9 years old	Amy	

35   110 cm

36   70 cm

37   110 cm

Answers **Year 4 - Level 4**

1	2.6, 2.9, 3.0, 3.2
2	52, 12, 20
3	1600, 35900, 18, 45
4	45 minutes
5	0.24, 0.4, 3.04, 4
6	4 pineapples
7	14
8	96
9	21 x 4 = 84
10	2
11	12
12	4
13	650
14	40, 48, 24
	5, 8, 4
	28, 32, 21
	4, 8, 7
15	16 girls
16	£3.84
17	33p
18	(5 , 4)
19	451
20	5840
21	12 pots
22	14.4
23	3.61
24	17.4

25

26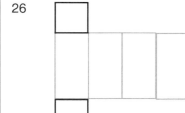

27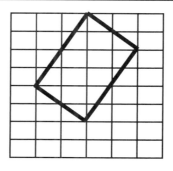

28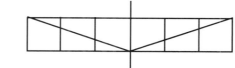

29

30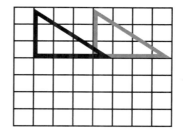

31 *The distance from Paris to London ....kilometres*
The length of a pencil .....centimetres
The length of the classroom .....metres

32 0.6 kg

33 Area = 25cm²   Perimeter = 20cm

34 6.40 pm

35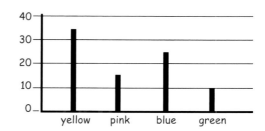

36 Monday and Friday

37 13 children

38 mode = 15   range = 9

APP Mathematics - Gap analysis for group and individual target setting

APP Year 4 Level 2   Date: Group:

			Names																
MA2	Qu.1	Count sets of objects reliably																	
	Qu.2	Order numbers up to 100																	
	Qu.3	Recognise sequences including odd/even																	
	Qu.4	Recognise sequences including odd/even																	
	Qu.5	Recognise sequences including odd/even																	
	Qu.6	Begin to use halves and quarters																	
	Qu.7	Begin to use halves and quarters																	
	Qu.8	Begin to use halves and quarters																	
	Qu.9	Begin to use halves and quarters																	
	Qu.10	Explore concept of half of a shape																	
	Qu.11	Explore concept of half of a shape																	
	Qu.12	Use subtraction as the inverse of addition																	
	Qu.13	Use subtraction as the inverse of addition																	
	Qu.14	Use halving to 'undo' doubling & vice versa																	
	Qu.15	Use halving to 'undo' doubling & vice versa																	
	Qu.16	Use addition and subtraction facts to 10																	
	Qu.17	Use addition and subtraction facts to 10																	
	Qu.18	Solve problems mentally involving money																	
	Qu.19	Solve problems mentally involving measure																	
	Qu.20	Chose appropriate operation solving problems																	
	Qu.21	Chose appropriate operation solving problems																	
	Qu.22	Solve problems involving money and measures																	
	Qu.23	Solve problems involving money and measures																	
	Qu.24	Record number work in writing																	
MA3	Qu.25	Name common 2D and 3D shapes																	
	Qu.26	Describe shape properties e.g sides/corners																	
	Qu.27	Describe shape properties e.g sides/corners																	
	Qu.28	Describe shape properties e.g sides/corners																	
	Qu.29	Describe the position of objects																	
	Qu.30	Distinguish between straight/turning movements																	
	Qu.31	Recognise right angles in turns																	
	Qu.32	Understand measurement of turn																	
	Qu.33	Use units to measure length and mass																	
	Qu.34	Begin to use days of the week/other measures																	
MA4	Qu.35	Sort/classify using more than one criterion																	
	Qu.36	Understand vocabulary relating to data																	
	Qu.37	Collect, sort and test data																	
	Qu.38	Record results in block graphs																	
	Qu.39	Communicate findings using block graphs																	

		APP Mathematics - Gap analysis for group and individual target setting

APP Mathematics - Gap analysis for group and individual target setting

APP Year 4 Level 3 Date: Group:

		Names
Qu.1	Order numbers up to 1000	
Qu.2	Round off to nearest 100	
Qu.3	Recognise negative temperatures	
Qu.4	Recognise negative temperatures	
Qu.5	Recognise a wider range of sequences	
Qu.6	Recognise a wider range of sequences	
Qu.7	Recognise fractions of a whole	
Qu.8	Recognise equivalent fractions	
Qu.9	Use decimal notation in money	
Qu.10	Derive division facts from multiplication facts	
Qu.11	Begin to understand the 'equals' sign	
Qu.12	Add/subtract 2 digit numbers mentally	
Qu.13	Add/subtract 2 digit numbers mentally	
Qu.14	Use mental recall of 2, 3, 4, 5 and 10 x tables	
Qu.15	Use mental recall of 2, 3, 4, 5 and 10 x tables	
Qu.16	Use mental recall of add./sub. facts to 20	
Qu.17	Solve problems with possible remainders	
Qu.18	Solve problems using multiplication	
Qu.19	Add/sub. 3 digit numbers in written methods	
Qu.20	Add/sub. 3 digit numbers in written methods	
Qu.21	x 2 digit numbers by 2, 3, 4, 5 and 10	
Qu.22	Divide 2 digit numbers by 2, 3, 4, 5 and 10	
Qu.23	Divide 2 digit numbers that give remainders	
Qu.24	Identify 2D shapes with right angles	
Qu.25	Classify 2D shapes using math. properties	
Qu.26	Classify 3D shapes using math. properties	
Qu.27	Recognise nets of 3D shapes	
Qu.28	Recognise shapes in different orientations	
Qu.29	Reflect shapes in a mirror line	
Qu.30	Describe position and movement	
Qu.31	Use standard and non-standard units	
Qu.32	Use standard units of time	
Qu.33	Use a wider range of measures	
Qu.34	Use a Carroll diagram to sort/classify info.	
Qu.35	Interpret information from bar charts	
Qu.36	Interpret information from bar charts	
Qu.37	Interpret information from bar charts	

A3

A4

APP Mathematics - Gap analysis for group and individual target setting

APP Year 4 Level 4   Date: Group:

			Names																	
MA2	Qu.1	Recognise and describe number patterns																		
	Qu.2	Recognise and describe multiples																		
	Qu.3	Use place value to x or ÷ by 10 or 100																		
	Qu.4	Use fractions to describe portions of a whole																		
	Qu.5	Order decimals to 3 decimal places																		
	Qu.6	Begin to understand simple ratio																		
	Qu.7	Use inverse operations																		
	Qu.8	Use inverse operations																		
	Qu.9	Use inverse operations																		
	Qu.10	Use inverse operations																		
	Qu.11	Understand the use of brackets in calculations																		
	Qu.12	Derive division facts from x table facts																		
	Qu.13	Use a range of mental computations																		
	Qu.14	Quickly recall x and ÷ facts up to 10 x 10																		
	Qu.15	Solve problems with/without calculator																		
	Qu.16	Check the reasonableness of results																		
	Qu.17	Begin to use simple word formulae																		
	Qu.18	Use co-ordinates in 1st quadrant																		
	Qu.19	Use efficient written methods for number cal.																		
	Qu.20	Use efficient written methods for number cal.																		
	Qu.21	Use efficient written methods for number cal.																		
	Qu.22	Add/subtract decimals to 2 places																		
	Qu.23	Add/subtract decimals to 2 places																		
	Qu.24	Multiply simple decimal by a single digit																		
MA3	Qu.25	Use the properties of 2D shapes																		
	Qu.26	Make 3D models by linking given faces/edges																		
	Qu.27	Draw 2D shapes in different orientations																		
	Qu.28	Reflect simple shapes in a mirror line																		
	Qu.29	Rotate a shape about its centre																		
	Qu.30	Translate shapes horizontally or vertically																		
	Qu.31	Choose/use appropriate units of measurement																		
	Qu.32	Interpret numbers on measuring instruments																		
	Qu.33	Find areas/perimeters of shapes																		
	Qu.34	Use units of time																		
MA4	Qu.35	Construct simple line graphs																		
	Qu.36	Interpret frequency diagrams																		
	Qu.37	Use diagrams to record sorting/classifying																		
	Qu.38	Use mode and range to describe sets of data																		